To Kate,
With love,
Uncle Bob & Aunt Marilee
Christmas 2016

# The Little Turtle

# The Little Turtle

*(A Recitation for Martha Wakefield, Three Years Old)*

a poem *by* Vachel Lindsay

illustrations *by* George Colin

VACHEL LINDSAY ASSOCIATION

2012

Copyright ©2012
Vachel Lindsay Association

ISBN: 978-0-615-70526-2

Printed in Canada

The Vachel Lindsay Association (VLA) wishes to express its thanks to Nicholas Cave Lindsay for permission to reprint his father's work.

Book design and book typesetting by Judy Gilats

# Foreword

An Open Letter to the
Students of Vachel Lindsay School

*October 2000*

When I was two years old my family spent a year's furlough with my mother's family at 603 South 5th Street. There we lived with Grandmother and Grandfather Lindsay and Uncle Vachel. I was not only young but also new to American ways. Fortunately, I had an older sister, Catharine, who, being almost five, knew everything.

Uncle Vachel was a tease, finding all kinds of creatures in corners and closets. When he called me to find them too, I'd always moved too fast or too noisily so the creatures never let me see them.

Uncle Vachel brought home a turtle from the Five & Ten for Catharine and me. It was about the size of the back of my hand. And very lively. Grandmother put a round wooden wash tub on the kitchen porch, which my father filled with water. We put the turtle in the tub and he swam wonderfully. But he needed a resting place so Dad found a large stone in the back yard and put it in the center of the tub. Sometimes the sun hit the water and when the turtle swam, the sun made silver snakes swim on the bottom of the tub. I looked and looked.

My uncle liked to make poems and he made one for me. He called it "The Little Turtle, for Martha Wakefield, two years old." Then he and my sister Catharine and our grandparents taught me the poem.

One day when Uncle Vachel was away, giving a recital of his poetry to many people in another city, he sang them my poem and said I, Martha, could sing all of it, and that I was two years old. A woman in the audience stood up and said, "Mr. Lindsay, no two-year-old could recite that poem." So Uncle Vachel bowed very low and said, "In that case, Madame, she is three." He came home and told us all about it. And in his books, though the subtitle read "The Little Turtle is for Martha Wakefield, three years old," I always knew that was wrong.

When I grew up I became a teacher of Head Start and kindergarten. I loved giving "my" children my poem, but I never told them it was mine. Because when they learned it, it should be theirs. Now I understand that a new school is going to be opened in Springfield and it is to be named for Uncle Vachel. And now perhaps a teacher will be giving "The Little Turtle" to many more children. This makes me very happy indeed.

> Martha Wakefield Falcone
> *no longer 3*

*Martha Wakefield Falcone, a niece of Vachel Lindsay, wrote the above letter to the students of the new Vachel Lindsay School on the occasion of the school's dedication. In an accompanying note, she wrote, "Vachel would be delighted with a school named Lindsay!" The children and faculty of the school were equally delighted to receive her correspondence.*

# The Little Turtle

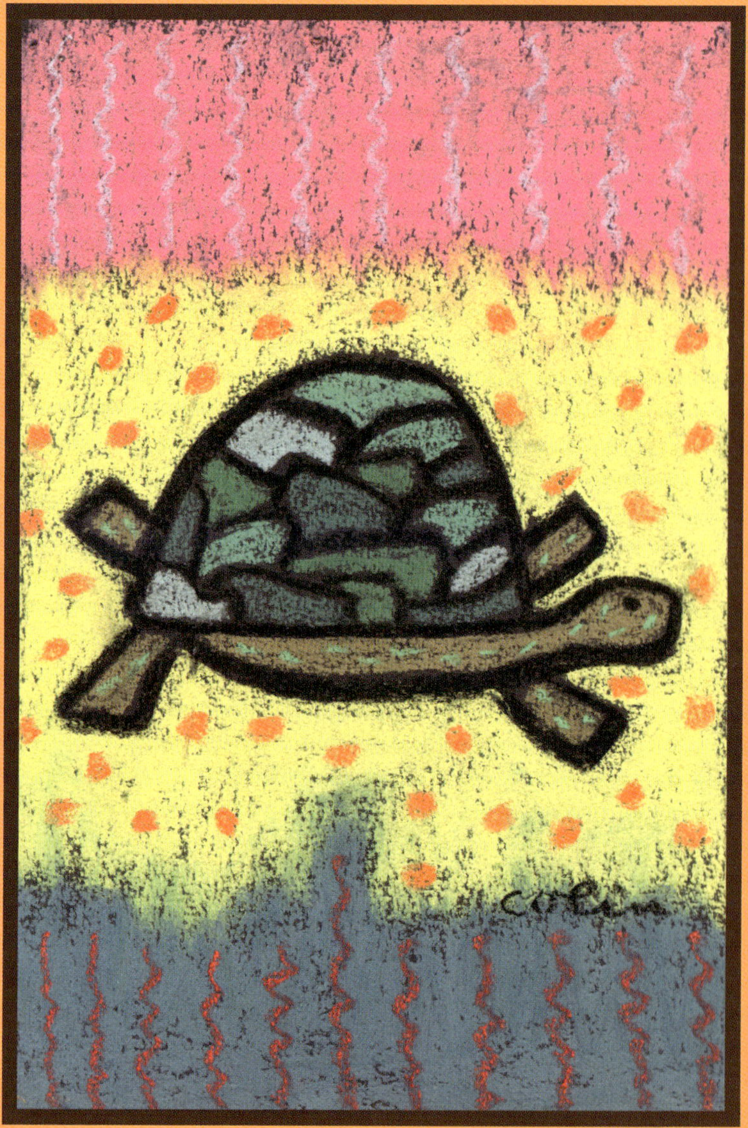

There was a little turtle.

He lived in a box.

He swam in a puddle.

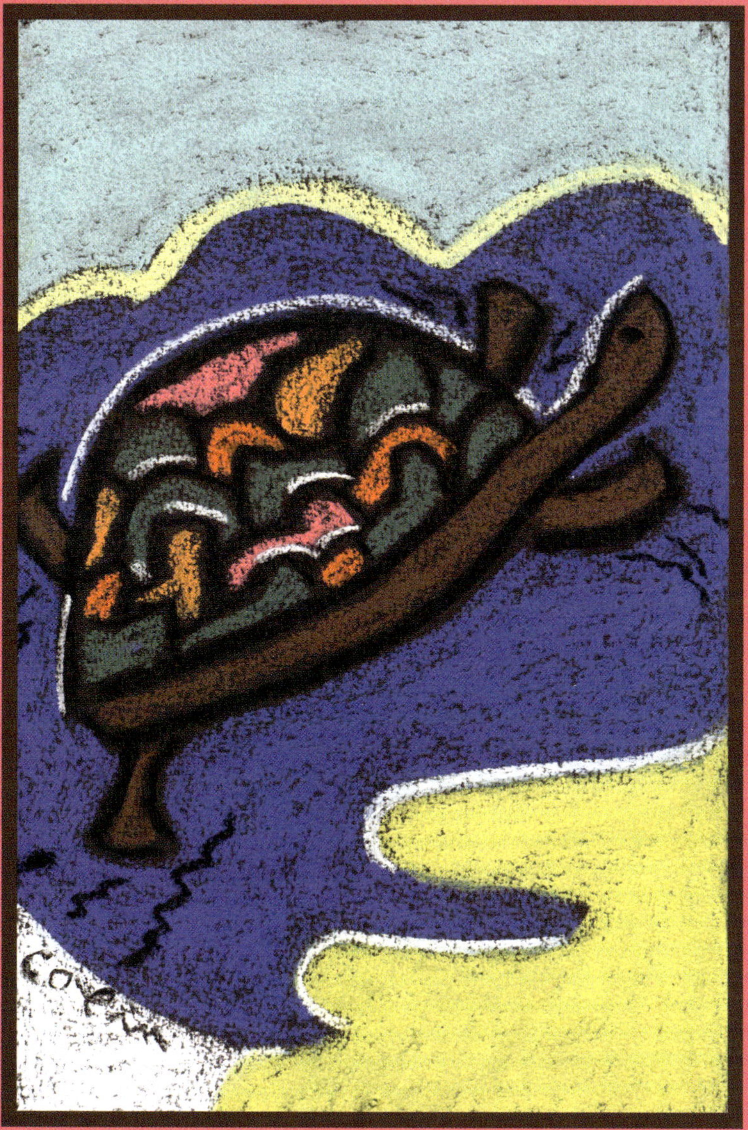

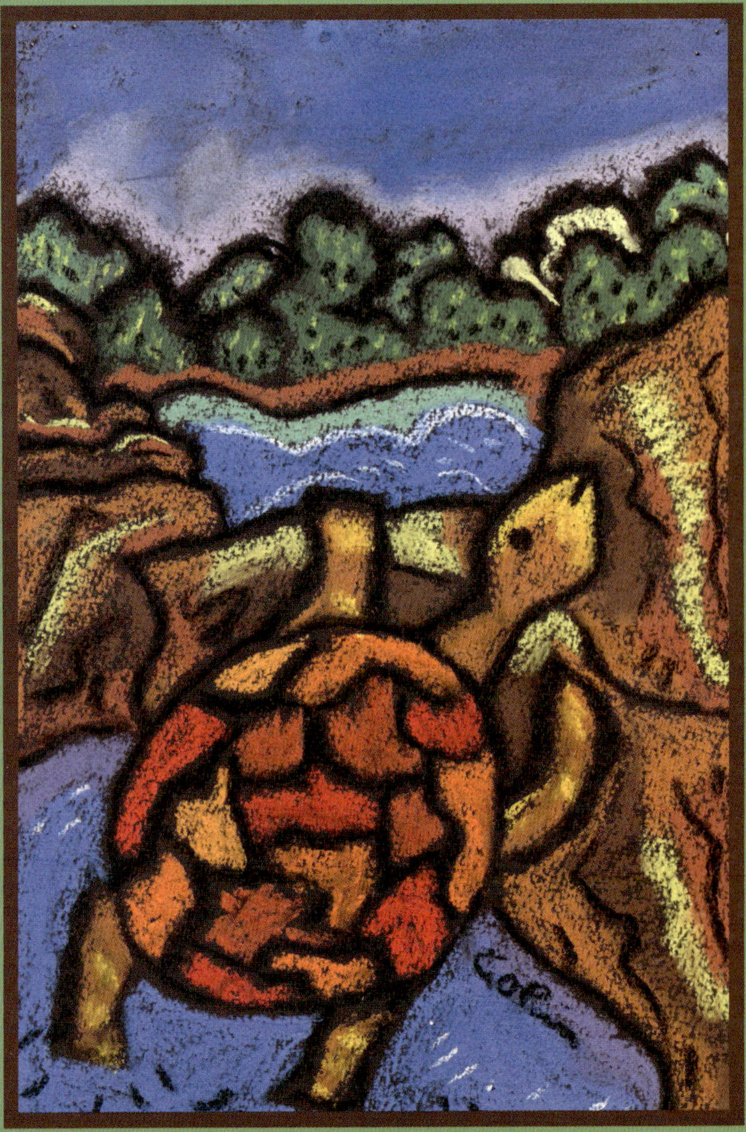

He climbed on the rocks.

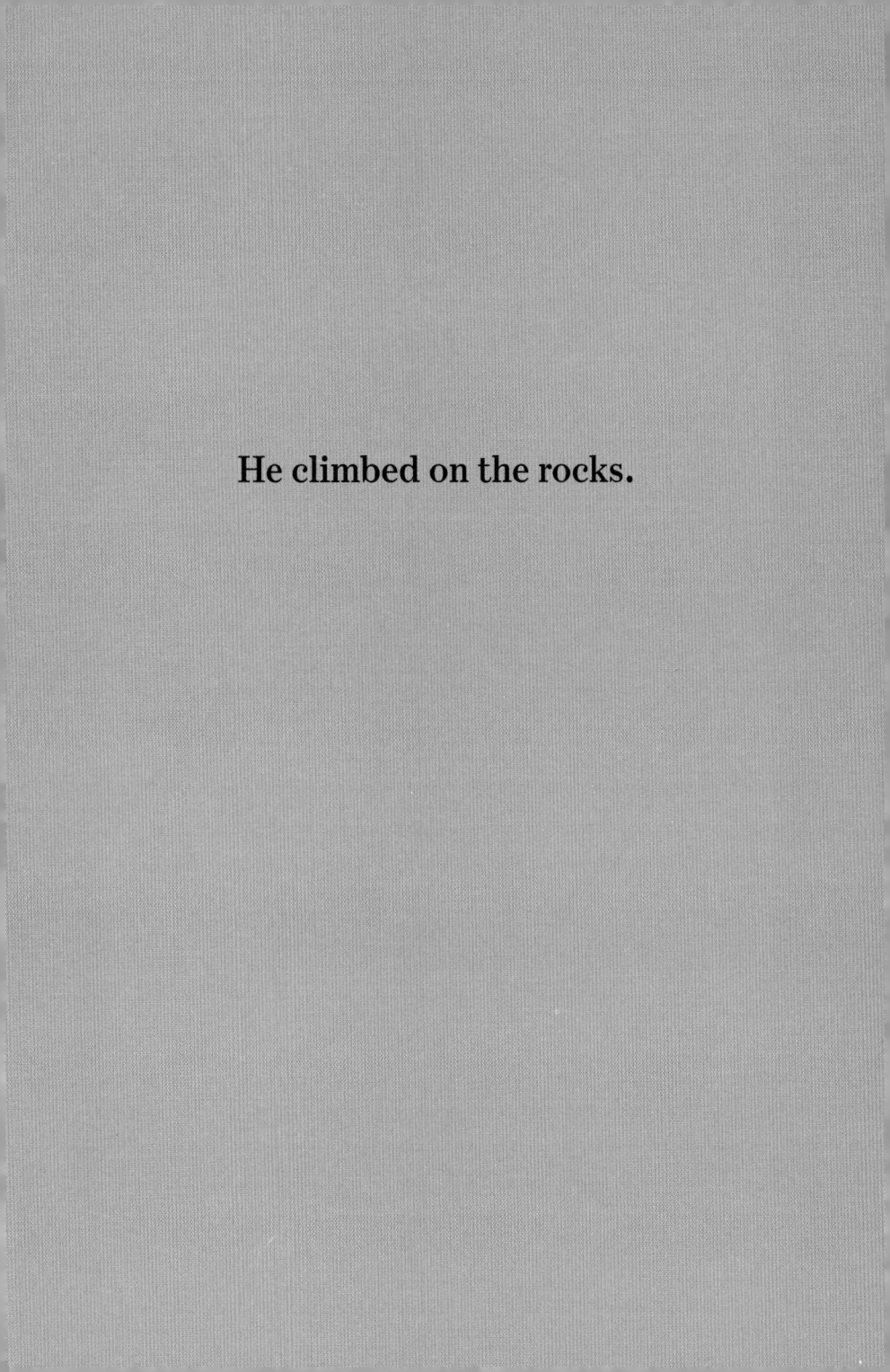

He snapped at a mosquito.

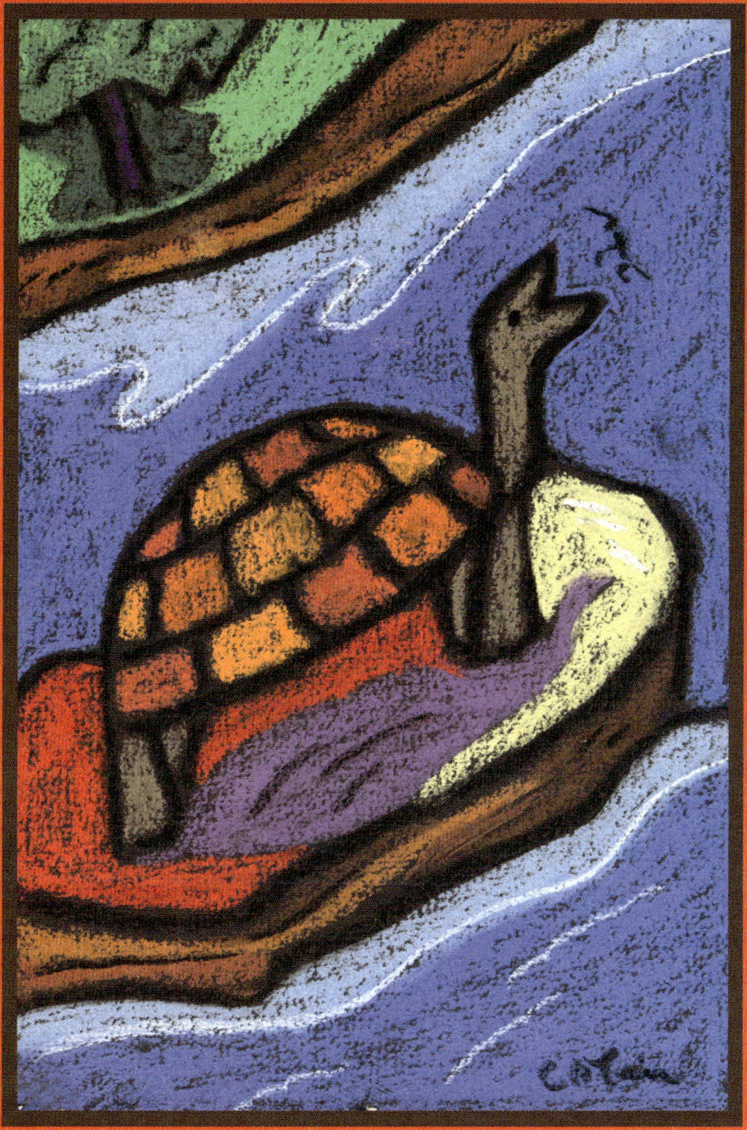

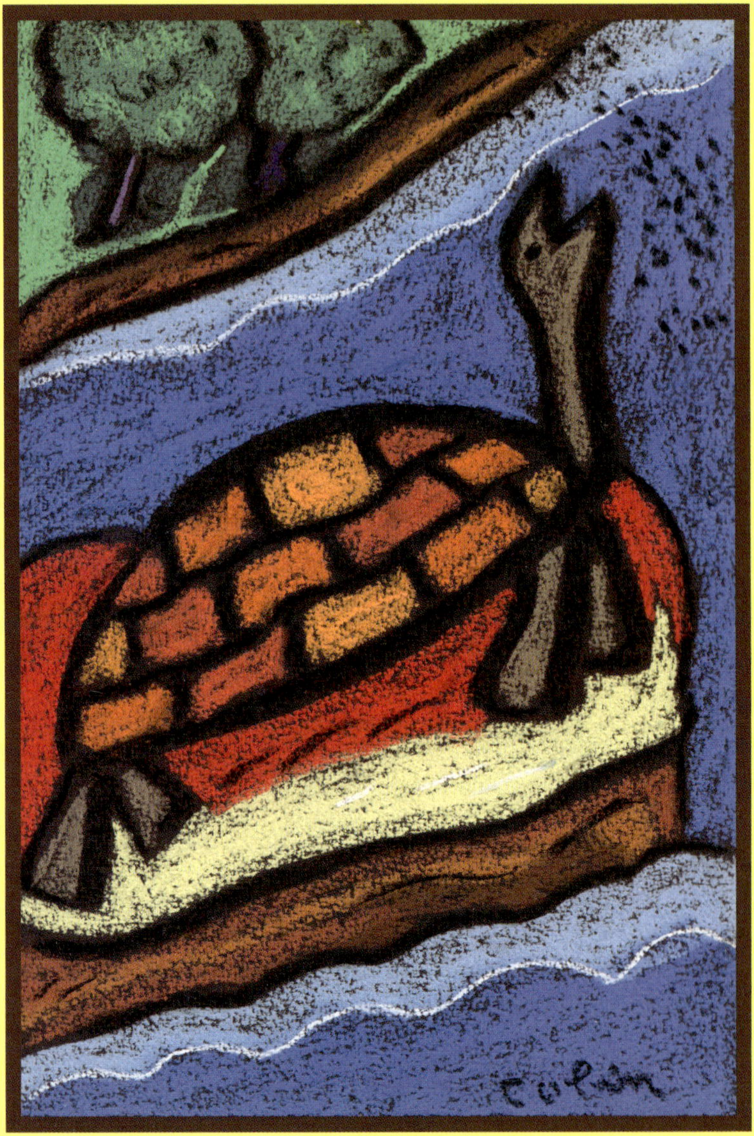

He snapped at a flea.

He snapped at a minnow.

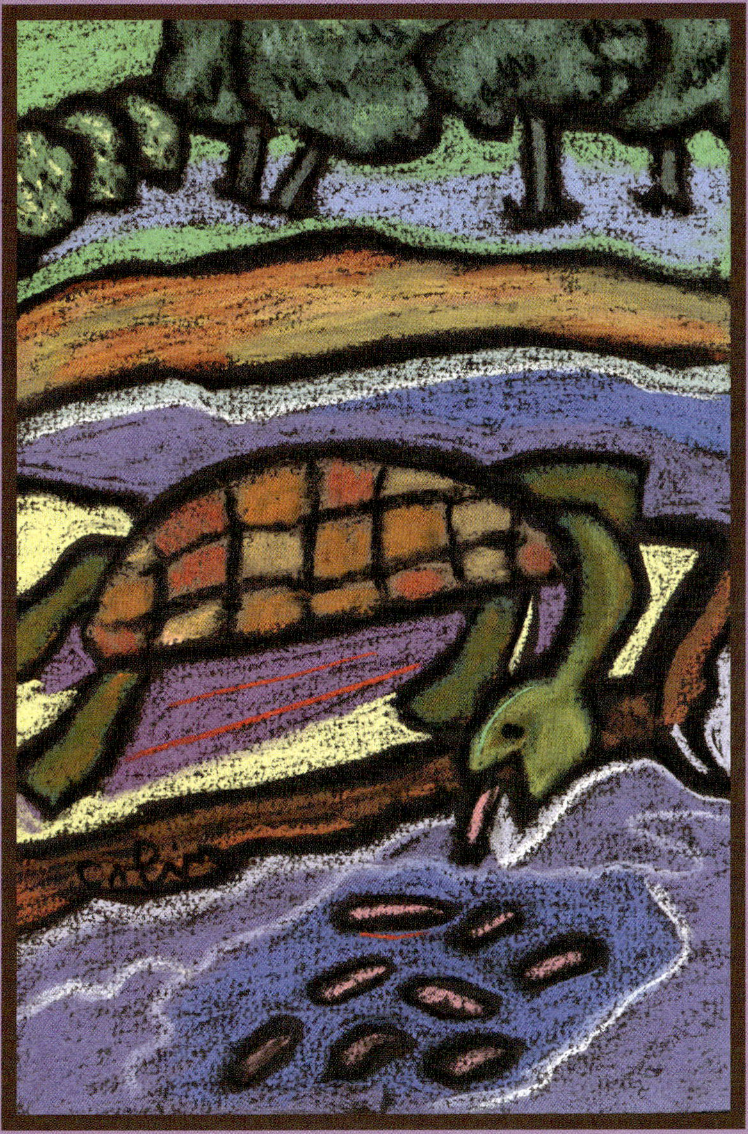

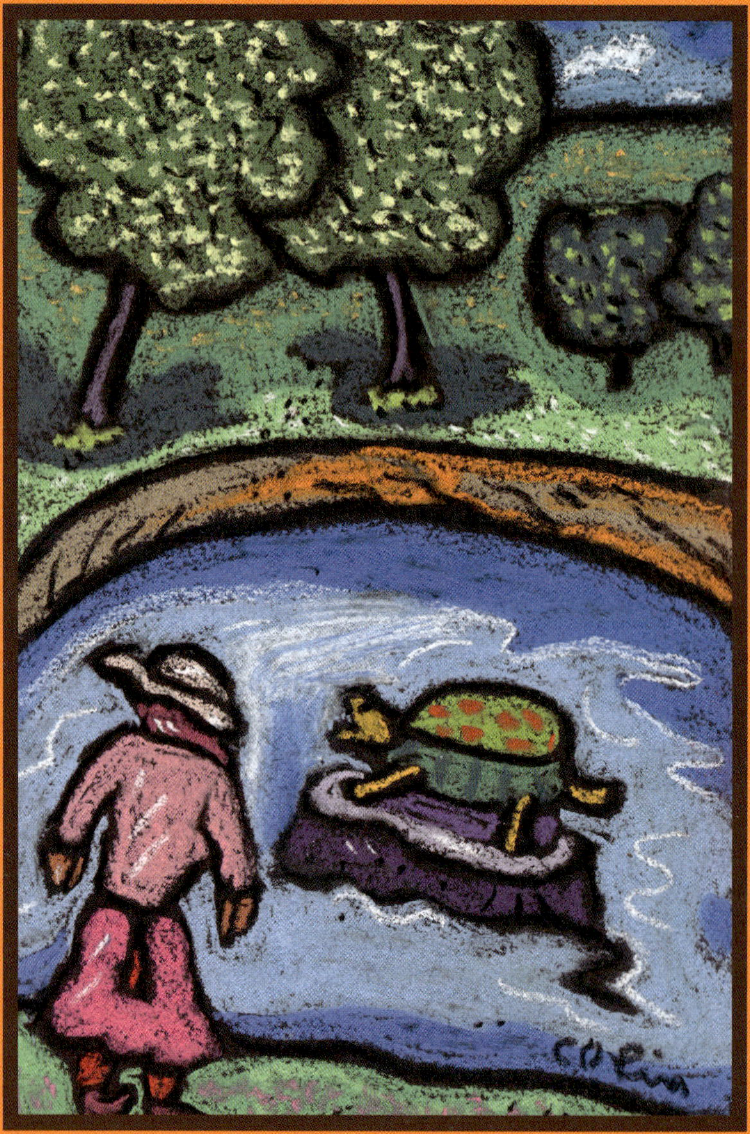

And he snapped at me.

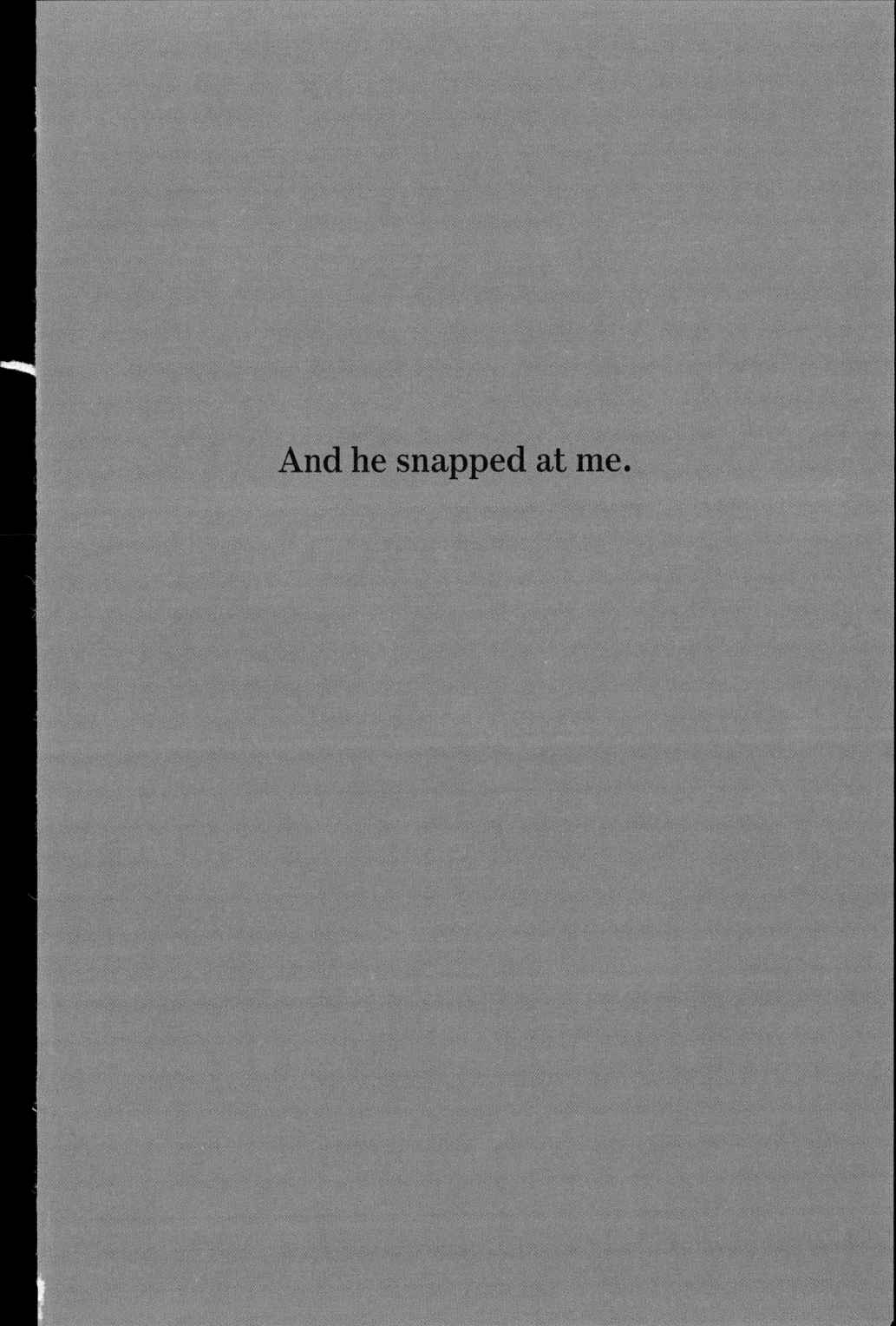

He caught the mosquito.

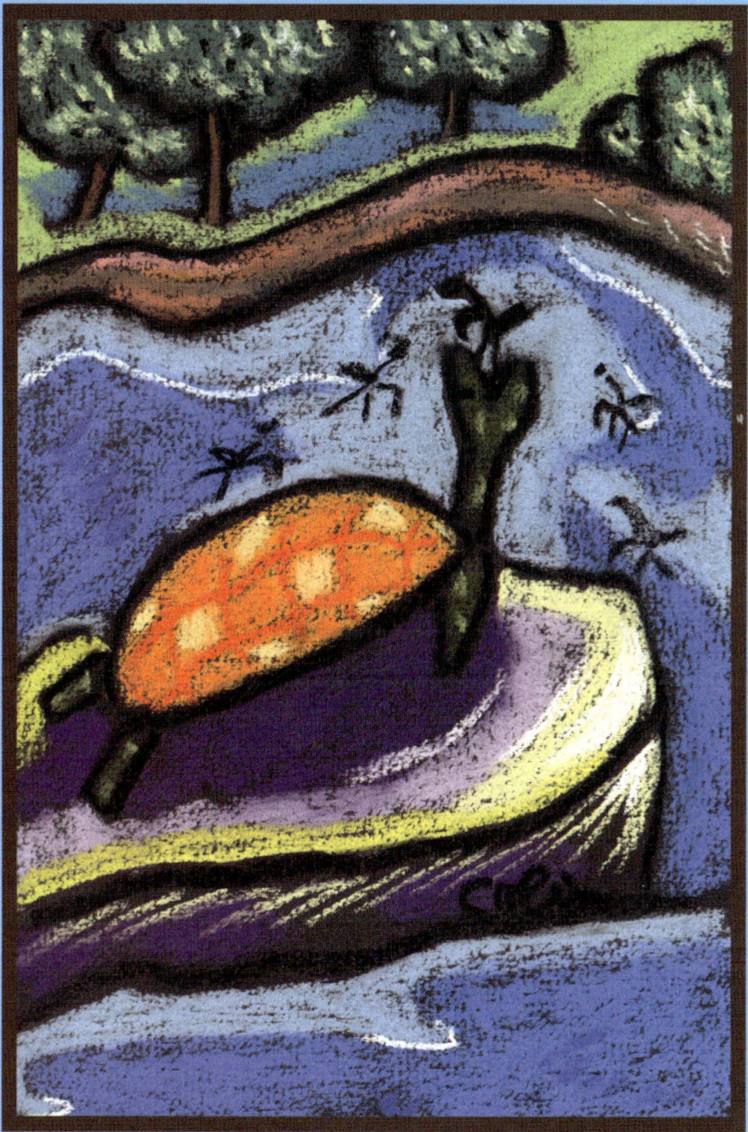

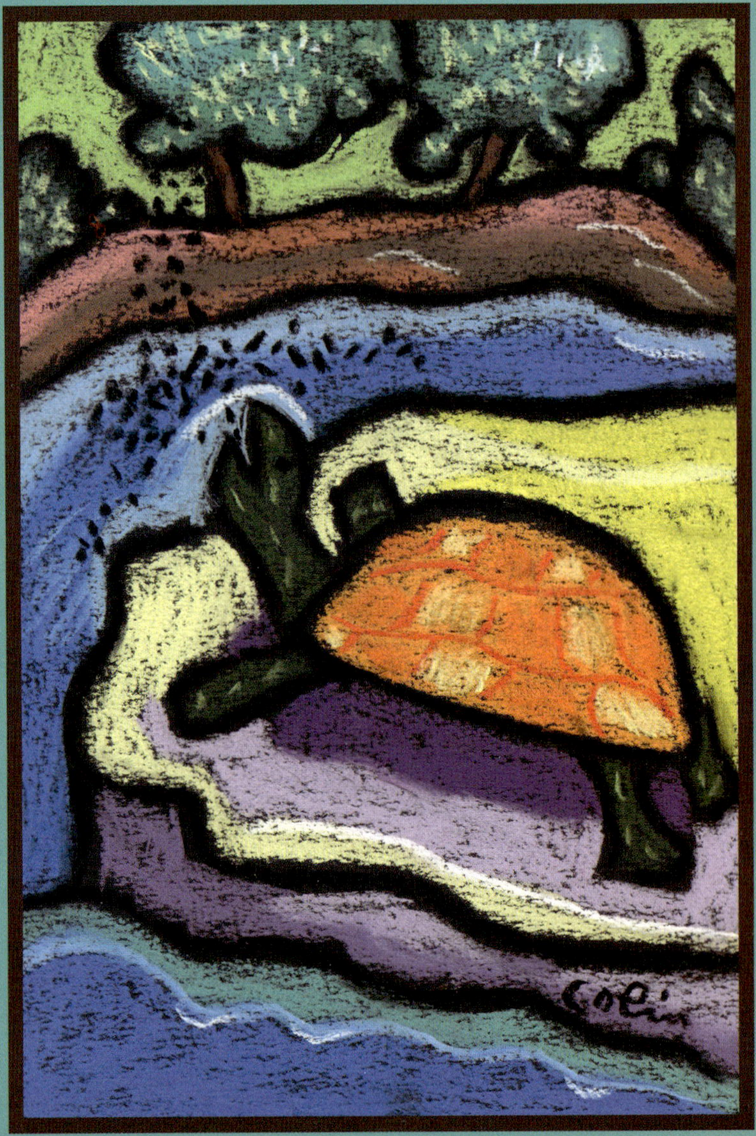
Colin

He caught the flea.

He caught the minnow.

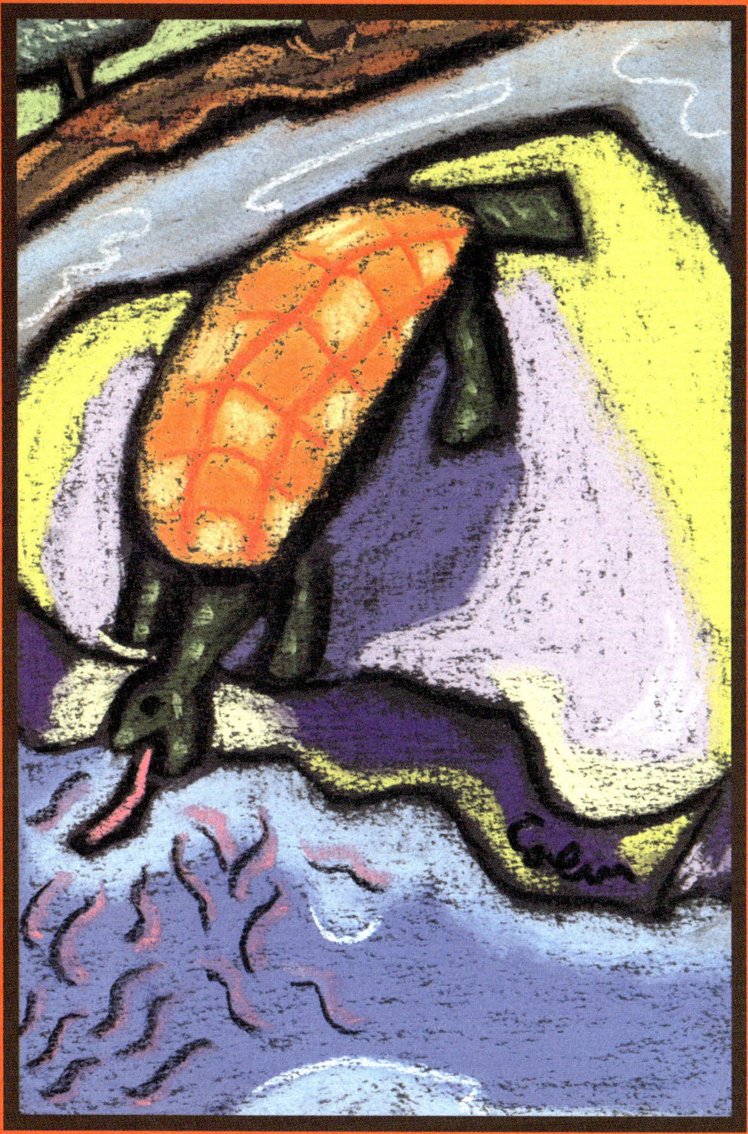

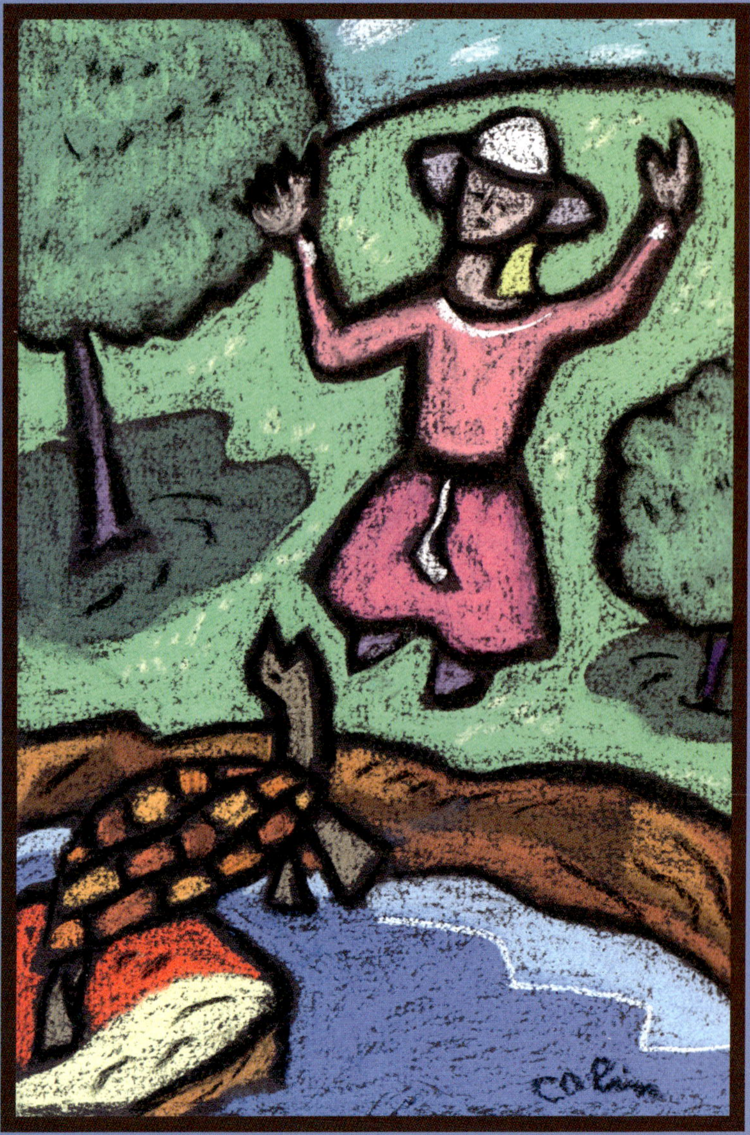

But he didn't catch me.

Nicholas Vachel Lindsay was born on November 10, 1879, in Springfield, Illinois. His high school English teacher, Susan Wilcox, inspired Vachel to dream and to write. Even though he started college to become a doctor, Vachel persuaded his parents to let him change course and study art. His parents eventually agreed, sending him to the Chicago Art Institute and the New York School of Art so he could follow his dream.

Another teacher, Robert Henri, told Vachel he was more a poet than a painter. Soon, Vachel was writing poems and tramping across the country—from Florida to Kentucky, New York to Ohio, Illinois to New Mexico—trading poems for a meal and a place to spend the night. So began the career of our country's most trailblazing prairie poet, whose poetry performances across America and England delighted audiences for decades.

Some of Vachel's best known poems include "General William Booth Enters into Heaven," "The Wedding of the Rose and the Lotus," and "Abraham Lincoln Walks at Midnight." However, many children first hear of Vachel through his lovely poem, "The Little Turtle."

After his death in 1931, Vachel Lindsay was buried at Oak Ridge Cemetery in Springfield, Illinois, near his hometown hero, Abraham Lincoln.

GEORGE COLIN was born in 1929 in Hollywood, California, but he has lived most of his life in Illinois. To help support his family, George left high school early and sacked flour at the Pillsbury Mills for over thirty years. However, he was always dreaming of art.

So in his spare time before and after he went to work, George created art. Unable to buy expensive canvas or paint, he often painted on paper he found in dumpsters behind local art stores and printing companies. George painted with children's watercolors, markers, house paint, and spray paint. Eventually he started working with chalk pastels, which is the medium he uses today.

George is well known in the world of folk art. Famous people from all over the world, such as Michael Jordan and Oprah Winfrey, have his work in their homes and offices. George and Winnie, his wife of almost fifty years, live in an old converted garage filled with George's work. They are quite a glorious pair.

At eighty-three years old, George is living his dream each day as he creates art in the little studio right off the highway in Salisbury, Illinois.